The Planets

by Marne Ventura

www.focusreaders.com

Copyright © 2023 by Focus Readers®, Lake Elmo, MN 55042. All rights reserved. No part of this book may be reproduced or utilized in any form or by any means without written permission from the publisher.

Focus Readers is distributed by North Star Editions:
sales@northstareditions.com | 888-417-0195

Produced for Focus Readers by Red Line Editorial.

Photographs ©: JPL-Caltech/Space Science Institute/NASA, cover, 1; JPL-Caltech/NASA, 4, 7, 19, 25, 27; NOAO/AURA/NSF/University of Colorado/JPL-Caltech/NASA, 8; Goddard/GSFC/NASA, 11; Voyager 2/JPL/NASA, 13; Johns Hopkins University Applied Physics Laboratory/Southwest Research Institute/JPL/NASA, 14–15, 29; iStockphoto, 16; JPL/NASA, 21; Cornell University/JPL/NASA, 22

Library of Congress Cataloging-in-Publication Data
Library of Congress Cataloging-in-Publication Data is available on the Library of Congress website.

ISBN
978-1-63739-247-8 (hardcover)
978-1-63739-299-7 (paperback)
978-1-63739-401-4 (ebook pdf)
978-1-63739-351-2 (hosted ebook)

Printed in the United States of America
Mankato, MN
082022

About the Author

Marne Ventura has written more than 100 books for children. She holds a master's degree in education from the University of California. Her favorite topics are nature; science, technology, engineering, and math (STEM); crafts; food; biographies; and health. Marne and her husband live on the central coast of California.

Table of Contents

CHAPTER 1
Life on Mars? 5

CHAPTER 2
What Is a Planet? 9

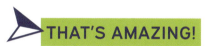
THAT'S AMAZING!
Pluto 14

CHAPTER 3
Exploring the Planets 17

CHAPTER 4
More Missions 23

Focus on the Planets • 28
Glossary • 30
To Learn More • 31
Index • 32

Chapter 1

Life on Mars?

People have long been curious about Mars. **NASA** scientists wanted to know if life ever existed on the planet. So, they sent a **rover** into space. In 2021, it landed on the red planet.

An illustration shows the Perseverance rover landing on Mars.

The rover drilled into the soil. Then it took samples. NASA planned to pick up the samples later. Then scientists planned to study the soil. They hoped to find signs of life from long ago.

Mars holds many mysteries. And it is not the only planet that

Life-forms need water to live. So, the Mars rover landed in a crater that was once the site of a lake.

 An illustration shows the Mars rover searching for signs of life.

scientists are studying. **Probes** have visited every planet in our **solar system**. Scientists have learned much. But there is always more to discover.

Chapter 2

What Is a Planet?

Our solar system started forming 4.6 billion years ago. At first, it was a giant cloud of dust and gas. Over time, gravity pulled the dust and gas together. This process created several huge balls in space.

 The solar system began as a massive cloud of dust and gas.

The biggest ball became a star. It is our Sun. The smaller balls became planets. Our solar system has one star and eight planets.

To be a planet, an object must follow three rules. It must **orbit** the Sun. It must be shaped like a ball. And it must clear its orbit. This

Did You Know?

Each planet orbits the Sun in an elliptical path. An ellipse is shaped like an oval.

 Earth is the third planet from the Sun.

means no other objects move in the same path.

There are four inner planets. They are Mercury, Venus, Earth, and Mars.

They are closer to the Sun than the outer planets are. The inner planets are made of rock and metal.

So far, Earth is the only planet where life has been found. Scientists say Earth is in the Goldilocks Zone. Earth is not too hot. And it is not too cold. Earth's distance from the Sun allows it to have liquid water. This water keeps plants and animals alive.

There are four outer planets. They are Jupiter, Saturn, Uranus,

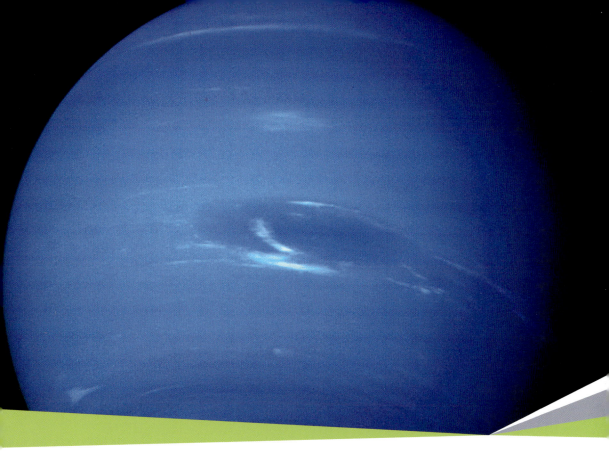

 Neptune is the farthest planet from the Sun.

and Neptune. They are much bigger than the inner planets. The outer planets are made of cold, swirling gases. Bits of rock and ice form rings around them.

THAT'S AMAZING!

Pluto

Pluto was discovered in 1930. For many years, scientists counted it as the ninth planet. But Pluto is much smaller than the other eight planets. And over time, scientists found other objects that were about the same size as Pluto.

In 2006, scientists came up with the three rules that planets must follow. Pluto does not meet the third rule. It has not cleared its orbit. So, Pluto is no longer called a planet. Instead, it is a dwarf planet.

A probe flew past Pluto in 2015.

Chapter 3

Exploring the Planets

From Earth, we can see five other planets with our eyes. For many years, those were the only planets people knew about. But in 1609, a scientist built a telescope. It made objects appear larger.

 Galileo Galilei used his telescope to discover four of Jupiter's moons.

Using telescopes, people could now see Neptune and Uranus. They could learn more about faraway objects.

In 1962, NASA launched the first spacecraft to another planet. Mariner 2 flew past Venus. It gathered **data** about the planet's

In 1971, Mariner 9 became the first spacecraft to orbit another planet. It gathered data about the atmosphere of Mars.

 Venus is covered by thick clouds.

hot, windy surface. In 1965, Mariner 4 flew past Mars. This was the first spacecraft to take up-close photos of another planet.

Pioneer 10 launched in 1972. It was NASA's first mission to the outer planets. The spacecraft flew past Jupiter. Its camera took hundreds of pictures.

Viking 1 and 2 launched in 1975. These spacecraft landed on Mars. They made maps of the planet's surface. They did experiments to search for life.

Voyager 1 and 2 were launched in 1977. They flew past Jupiter and Saturn. They sent back data

 Saturn's rings are made of bits of rock and ice.

about the gas giants. They found active volcanoes on one of Jupiter's moons. And they took photos of Saturn's rings.

21

Chapter 4

More Missions

Recent missions have taught scientists more about the planets. In 1997, the first rover landed on Mars. Two more rovers landed on the red planet in 2004. And a fourth landed in 2012.

 The Opportunity rover studied Mars from 2004 to 2018.

The rovers studied the surface of Mars. Scientists learned that Mars may have had liquid water long ago. They also found **molecules** that are the building blocks of life.

In 2004, a probe reached Saturn. It orbited the planet for 13 years. It studied Saturn's rings and moons.

Did You Know?

Exoplanets are planets beyond our solar system. Scientists have found thousands of exoplanets. And they find more every year.

 The Cassini probe crashed into Saturn at the end of its mission.

A probe began orbiting Venus in 2015. It studied the planet's weather. It looked for lightning, thick clouds, and active volcanoes.

25

In 2016, a probe reached Jupiter. It orbited the gas giant. The probe studied Jupiter's atmosphere. It measured temperature and moisture. Scientists hoped to learn more about how Jupiter formed.

In 2018, scientists sent a probe toward Mercury. They expected it to start orbiting the planet in 2025. Its goal was to learn about Mercury's surface. Another goal was to find out more about the planet's **magnetic field**.

 Jupiter is the largest planet in our solar system. The Juno probe started orbiting Jupiter in 2016.

Probes have taught us much about the planets. But scientists also hope to study other planets up close. So, NASA is working on plans to send humans to Mars.

FOCUS ON
The Planets

Write your answers on a separate piece of paper.

1. Write a letter to a friend describing what you learned about the search for life on Mars.

2. Which planet do you find most interesting? Why?

3. Which planets are gas giants?
   - A. the inner planets
   - B. the outer planets
   - C. the exoplanets

4. What might scientists learn if they find liquid water on a planet?
   - A. The planet might contain rock.
   - B. The planet might be made of gas.
   - C. The planet might support life.

5. What does **samples** mean in this book?

The rover drilled into the soil. Then it took samples.

    A. small pieces taken from a larger object
    B. probes that can travel to other planets
    C. machines that can break apart rocks

6. What does **missions** mean in this book?

Recent missions have taught scientists more about the planets. In 1997, the first rover landed on Mars.

    A. schools where people study science
    B. important tasks or operations
    C. people who study other planets

Answer key on page 32.

Glossary

data
Information collected to study or track something.

magnetic field
The space around an object (such as a moon or planet) in which its magnetic force can be detected.

molecules
Groups of atoms that are joined together.

NASA
The National Aeronautics and Space Administration, a part of the US government that focuses on space research and travel.

orbit
To repeatedly follow a curved path around another object because of gravity.

probes
Devices used to explore.

rover
A wheeled spacecraft that rolls across the surface of a planet or moon.

solar system
The Sun and all the objects that move around it, including planets, moons, asteroids, and comets.

To Learn More

BOOKS

Hirsch, Rebecca E. *Planets in Action (An Augmented Reality Experience)*. Minneapolis: Lerner Publications, 2020.

Huddleston, Emma. *Explore the Planets*. Minneapolis: Abdo Publishing, 2022.

Nargi, Lela. *Mysteries of Planets, Stars, and Galaxies*. North Mankato, MN: Capstone Press, 2021.

NOTE TO EDUCATORS

Visit **www.focusreaders.com** to find lesson plans, activities, links, and other resources related to this title.

Index

E
Earth, 11–12, 17

G
Goldilocks Zone, 12

J
Jupiter, 12, 20–21, 26

M
Mariner, 18–19
Mars, 5–6, 11, 18–20, 23–24, 27
Mercury, 11, 26

N
NASA, 5–6, 18, 20, 27
Neptune, 13, 18

P
Pioneer, 20
Pluto, 14
probes, 7, 24–27

R
rovers, 5–6, 23–24

S
Saturn, 12, 20–21, 24
solar system, 7, 9–10, 24
Sun, 10, 12

U
Uranus, 12, 18

V
Venus, 11, 18, 25
Viking, 20
Voyager, 20

Answer Key: 1. Answers will vary; **2.** Answers will vary; **3.** B; **4.** C; **5.** A; **6.** B